Famous Legends

The Legend of Robin Hood

By
Julia McDonnell

Gareth Stevens
PUBLISHING

Please visit our website, www.garethstevens.com. For a free color catalog of all our high-quality books, call toll free 1-800-542-2595 or fax 1-877-542-2596.

Cataloging-in-Publication Data

McDonnell, Julia.
The legend of Robin Hood / by Julia McDonnell.
p. cm. — (Famous legends)
Includes index.
ISBN 978-1-4824-2748-6 (pbk.)
ISBN 978-1-4824-2749-3 (6 pack)
ISBN 978-1-4824-2750-9 (library binding)
1. Robin Hood (Legendary character) — Legends — Juvenile literature. 2. Folklore England Juvenile literature. I. Title.
PZ8.1.M38 Ro 2016
398.22—d23

First Edition

Published in 2016 by
Gareth Stevens Publishing
111 East 14th Street, Suite 349
New York, NY 10003

Designer: Laura Bowen
Editor: Therese Shea

Photo credits: Cover, p. 1 James E. McConnell/The Bridgeman Art Library/Getty Images; cover, p. 1 (ribbon) barbaliss/Shutterstock.com; cover, p. 1 (leather) Pink Pueblo/Shutterstock.com; cover, pp. 1–32 (sign) Sarawut Padungkwan/Shutterstock.com; cover, pp. 1–32 (vines) vitasunny/Shutterstock.com; cover, pp. 1–32 (parchment) TyBy/Shutterstock.com; cover, pp. 1–32 (background) HorenkO/Shutterstock.com; p. 5 Culture Club/Hulton Archive/ Getty Images; p. 7 (main) Petra Mezei/Shutterstock.com; p. 7 (inset) C. Wilhelm/Stringer/Hulton Archive/Getty Images; p. 9 Paul Popper/Popperfoto/Getty Images; pp. 10, 19 Time Life Pictures/The LIFE Picture Collection/Getty Images; p. 11 Michael Warwick/Shutterstock.com; p. 13 Rischgitz/Stringer/Hulton Archive/Getty Images; p. 15 Hulton Archive/ Handout/Getty Images; p. 17 Arena Photo UK/Shutterstock.com; p. 21 © iStockphoto.com/duncan1890; p. 23 Daniel Maclise/Fine Art Photographic/Hulton Archive/Getty Images; p. 25 (main) © iStockphoto.com/ChrisCafferkey; p. 25 (inset) PNG crusade bot/Wikimedia Commons; p. 27 (main) Hulton Archive/Stringer/Moviepix/Getty Images; p. 27 (inset) LorenzoT/Wikimedia Commons; p. 29 WDG Photo/Shutterstock.com.

Printed in the United States of America

CPSIA compliance information: Batch #CS15GS: For further information contact Gareth Stevens, New York, New York at 1-800-542-2595.

Contents

Words in the glossary appear in **bold** type the first time they are used in the text.

A Hero and a Legend

Have you heard the saying "robbing the rich to give to the poor"? Do the words "Merry Men" or places like Sherwood Forest and Nottingham sound familiar? Do you think a thief could also be a hero? These are parts of the story of Robin Hood, a famous storybook hero and a man who may have really existed hundreds of years ago.

No one is sure exactly how or when the tales began, but they've grown into a **legend** that almost everyone knows.

The Inside Story

There are historic records of men who may have been the real Robin Hood. These include Robert Hod, Robin Hud, and Robard Hude. Robin Hood is sometimes also called Robin of Locksley.

Life was hard for the poor during Robin Hood's time, the **Middle Ages**. The poor often received no education and made everything they needed by hand. Many were farmers who raised crops and livestock.

The Outlaw of Sherwood

Robin Hood was said to have lived in England as early as the 1300s. He was kind, clever, and brave—and one of the best archers in the land. He was also an **outlaw**. The wicked Sheriff of Nottingham wanted badly to catch Robin Hood, the man who kept outsmarting him.

Robin and his partners, called the Merry Men, set up camp in Sherwood Forest. The thick forest offered them food, a hiding place, and money, thanks to a steady stream of travelers to rob. The outlaws shared their riches with anyone who needed them, though.

The Inside Story

Some say Robin became an outlaw by killing a castle guard who was chasing him. Others claim he was tricked into shooting one of the king's deer or blamed for stealing one.

Sherwood
Forest

Nottingham

ENGLAND

London

Tales of Robin Hood
are most often based
in Sherwood Forest
and Nottingham.

7

Little John

One day, Robin Hood tried to cross a log bridge at the same time as a large man. There wasn't room for both of them to cross the thin path. So, Robin **challenged** the stranger to a fight. The two men battled hard until Robin was knocked into the water!

The big man helped Robin up and asked where he could find Robin Hood. He said he wanted to join the Merry Men. Struck by his strength and kindness, Robin told him who he was. He and the man, called Little John, became good friends.

The Inside Story

The Merry Men included Little John, Will Stutely, Much the miller's son (sometimes called Dickon), **Friar** Tuck, and Will Scarlett (also spelled Scarlok or Scathelocke). The woman Robin loved, Maid Marian, was added to the stories later.

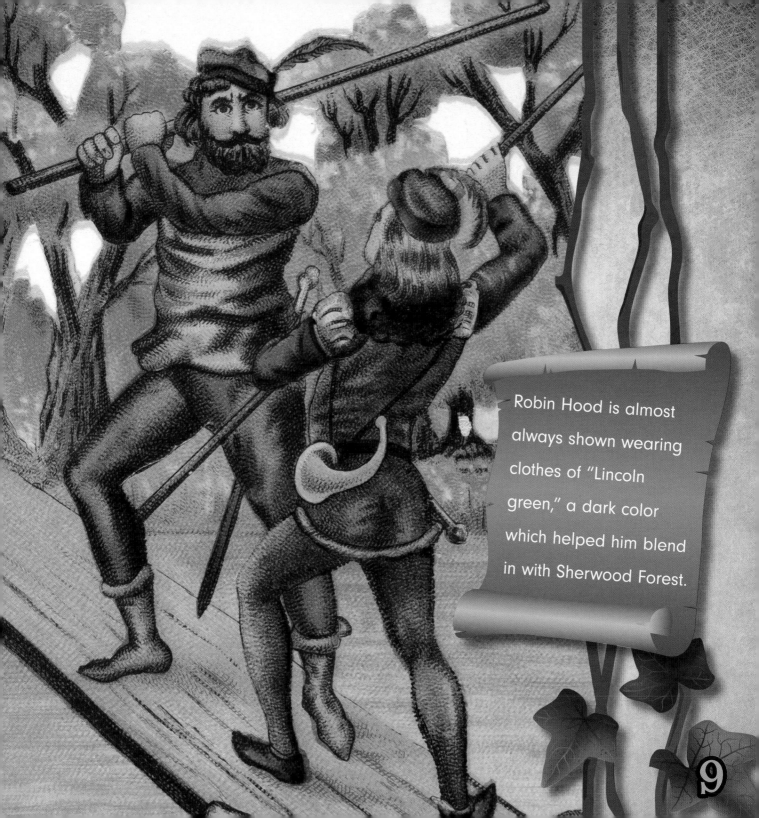

Robin Hood is almost always shown wearing clothes of "Lincoln green," a dark color which helped him blend in with Sherwood Forest.

Friar Tuck

Robin heard about the strength and archery skill of a friar named Tuck living in Sherwood Forest. Friar Tuck earned money by carrying people across a stream.

Robin found Tuck and asked to be carried across the water. When they reached the other side, Robin **demanded** to be brought back. The friar refused, and a fight began. Robin Hood was soon all wet! The men quickly realized they were evenly matched. Friar Tuck had proven himself, though. Robin asked him to join the Merry Men.

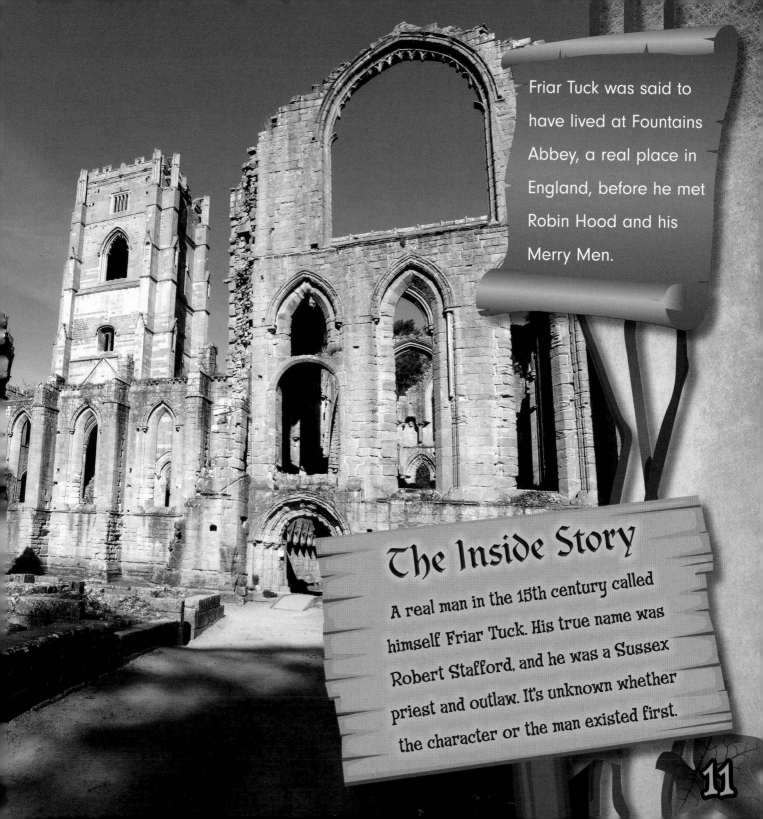

Friar Tuck was said to have lived at Fountains Abbey, a real place in England, before he met Robin Hood and his Merry Men.

The Inside Story

A real man in the 15th century called himself Friar Tuck. His true name was Robert Stafford, and he was a Sussex priest and outlaw. It's unknown whether the character or the man existed first.

Cheating a Cheater

Sir Richard was an honest knight who owed a lot of money to a greedy **abbot**. Robin Hood gave him the money, but had him test the abbot's kindness by asking for more time. The abbot refused, thinking he could claim the knight's castle and land instead. But Sir Richard surprised him with the amount owed and was freed from his **debt**.

The next time the abbot traveled through Sherwood Forest, Robin demanded payment—the amount he had given to Sir Richard. Robin got his money back!

The Inside Story

Sometimes the Merry Men invited rich travelers to feasts. After, Robin demanded money as payment.

The Merry Men stopped travelers and asked how much money they carried. If the person answered truthfully, they were allowed to keep it. If they lied, Robin took it all.

A Mysterious Butcher

Robin Hood looked for ways to help the poor—and ways to fool the greedy Sheriff of Nottingham. One day, Robin **disguised** himself and set up a stall in the market. He sold meat at low prices and gave it away to the very poor.

When the sheriff demanded that he pay taxes, Robin offered to show him his secret herds (which were really the king's animals). Once they entered Sherwood Forest, the Merry Men forced the sheriff to hand over his money. Tricked by Robin, the sheriff rode back to Nottingham, angrier than ever.

The Inside Story

At that time, England was divided into areas called shires, and each shire had its own sheriff. He had jobs such as carrying out laws and collecting taxes.

Deer were common in England's forests. If anyone hunted the king's personal herd, they could get in serious trouble. Robin Hood did it anyway and shared the meat with others.

15

A Close Call

One day, the sheriff caught Will Stutely, one of Robin Hood's Merry Men. Will was sentenced to be hanged! Robin hatched a plan to save him. When the townspeople gathered to watch the hanging, the outlaws blended into the crowd. A stranger stepped forward, telling the sheriff that he was the hangman.

However, at the last moment, the hangman threw off his cloak—it was Robin! He cut Will loose, while the other Merry Men fought off the sheriff's guards. They stole the guards' horses and escaped into Sherwood Forest safely.

This is a bronze statue of Friar Tuck, Little John, and Will Stutely in Nottingham today.

17

The Sheriff's Plan Backfires

The sheriff held an archery contest hoping that Robin Hood—the famed archer—would want to enter. Robin did enter, but in disguise. One archer hit the target's bull's-eye, but the contest wasn't over yet. Robin won by splitting the arrow in half with his own! The sheriff presented the disguised Robin with a golden arrow.

Later, Robin wanted to let the sheriff know he'd been tricked. So, he shot the golden arrow through the sheriff's window with a note attached, telling him who the winner really was.

The Inside Story

King Edward III (ruled 1327–1377) made archery practice for British men required by law since archers were needed in the army. The best archers could shoot up to 16 arrows in a minute!

The longbow was the most common weapon during the Middle Ages. A longbow is almost as tall as an archer!

Robin Gets Tricked

England had a ruler at this time, King Richard, but he was away fighting a **Crusade**. When Richard finally returned, he heard of the sheriff's illegal deeds and bullying ways as well as Robin Hood's bravery, kindness, and unselfishness.

Richard disguised himself as a rich friar and entered Sherwood Forest. As expected, the Merry Men stopped him. They surprised him with a feast and an archery contest. When Robin missed the target, his punishment was to be struck by their guest. The stranger was strong enough to knock Robin to the ground!

The Inside Story

While King Richard was away, his brother Prince John ruled. John wasn't well liked, and people who worked for him—like the sheriff—got away with breaking laws and making themselves rich.

Artists often painted King Richard I on the battlefield. Tales of his bravery led him to be called "Richard the Lion-Hearted."

21

The Gift of Freedom

The Merry Men laughed at the sight of their leader on the ground. Their laughter turned to shock when the visitor pulled off his friar's cloak to show who he truly was. They knelt down in front of their king.

King Richard offered everyone **pardons** and told them news of their good deeds for the poor had spread far and wide. Robin no longer had to hide from the sheriff, and he could serve a king he respected. Best of all, he could marry his love, Maid Marian. His days as an outlaw were over!

The Inside Story

Some tales end with the death of Robin Hood. Wounded and sick, he shot an arrow through the window of his room and asked his friends to bury him where it landed.

The Merry Men were shocked they had tried to rob King Richard! However, the king laughed and asked them to be his royal archers.

A Real Robin?

Robin Hood has been described as a nobleman, outlaw, robber, farmer, hunter, and more. There probably wasn't a real man named Robin Hood who was and did everything the stories say.

The character might have been created to appeal to lower classes who felt powerless to better their lives. Another possibility is that the **ballads** of Robin's adventures were created for and sung to rich people. As the story has changed over the years, the deeds and features of real men in history may have been added.

The Inside Story

As far as historians know, the name "Robin Hood" first appeared in writing in 1377. However, most of the tales were probably created in the 1400s.

It's said that Robin Hood and his Merry Men used the hollow trunk of the Major Oak in Sherwood Forest, shown here, as a hiding place.

Robin Hood ballad

Seen on Screen

The original Robin Hood ballads had plenty of unpleasant parts, including crimes and murders. Some of those parts have been dropped to make the stories more enjoyable today.

At the movies, a silent film of Robin Hood came out in 1922. It was the first of many movies about the hero, including *The Adventures of Robin Hood* (1938), *Robin Hood: Prince of Thieves* (1991), and even a Disney cartoon called *Robin Hood* (1973). There have been several Robin Hood TV shows as well.

The Inside Story

In the 1973 Disney cartoon, Robin Hood is a fox. This fits perfectly with Robin's tricky character in the stories.

Lego Robin Hood

Errol Flynn, shown here in *The Adventures of Robin Hood*, was one of the most famous actors to play Robin Hood.

Robin Hood Lives On

It doesn't seem to matter whether Robin Hood was a real man or how the tales began. The stories have lasted for centuries.

Characters and story elements changed along the way, but the ideals have stayed the same. The acts of fighting injustice, helping the poor, living a life of freedom, and valuing friendships appeal to many people, no matter the time period. As long as Robin Hood stands for all those things, his story will continue to be told for years to come.

The Inside Story

People around the world have tales of heroes who "right the wrongs" of the unjust, such as Korea's Hong Gil-dong and Germany's Klaus Störtebeker.

A statue of Robin Hood in Nottingham pays respect to the hero.

Glossary

abbot: the head of a monastery, a place where religious men called monks live together

ballad: a poem or song that tells a story

challenge: to test abilities

Crusade: one of the wars from the 11th to the 13th century in which Christians fought Muslims for control of the city of Jerusalem in the Middle East

debt: an amount of money owed

demand: to ask a question in a forceful way

disguise: to wear clothes or other things so that people will not recognize someone. Also, the clothes worn.

friar: one of a group of men who is poor and studies or teaches about Christianity

legend: a story that has been passed down for many, many years that's unlikely to be true

Middle Ages: a time in European history from about 500 to about 1500

outlaw: a person who has broken the law and who is hiding or running away to avoid punishment

pardon: an act of officially saying that someone guilty of a crime will be allowed to go free and unpunished

For More Information

Books

Calcutt, David. *Robin Hood.* Cambridge, MA: Barefoot Books, 2012.

McFadden, Deanna. *Robin Hood.* New York, NY: Sterling Children's Books, 2013.

Shepard, Aaron, Anne L. Watson, & Jennifer Tanner. *Robin Hood: A Graphic Novel.* North Mankato, MN: Stone Arch Books, 2014.

Websites

Robin Hood
britannia.com/history/rhood/
Explore the world of Robin Hood by taking a tour of famous places in the stories.

Robin Hood and His Historical Context
www.bbc.co.uk/history/british/middle_ages/robin_01.shtml
Learn about the facts and myths behind the legend of Robin Hood.

Robin Hood: The Facts and the Fiction
www.robinhoodlegend.com
Find information about the ballads, places, characters, and other details linked to the tales.

Index